SCIENCE EXPERIMENTS
Light and Sound

Om Books International

Om Books International

Reprinted in 2025

Corporate & Editorial Office
A-12, Sector 64, Noida 201 301
Uttar Pradesh, India
Phone: +91 120 477 4100
Email: editorial@ombooks.com
Website: www.ombooksinternational.com

Sales Office
107, Ansari Road, Darya Ganj
New Delhi 110 002, India
Phone: +91 11 4000 9000
Email: sales@ombooks.com
Website: www.ombooks.com

ISBN: 978-93-52763-09-2

Printed in India

10 9 8 7 6 5 4 3

CONTENTS

Duration of Experiment

5 mins

This icon indicates approximately how long the experiment will take, including the set-up time.

Difficulty Level

The black bars in this icon indicate level of difficulty in doing this experiment with one icon depicting the least level of difficulty.

Adult Supervision

This icon indicates that parental supervision is required. Always have an adult beside you.

NOTE: All activities and experiments described in this book should be ideally performed with adult supervision. Parents and guardians are advised to oversee the children and assist them with any difficult or potentially harmful tools. Common sense and discretion are advised. The publisher does not assume any responsibility for any injuries or damages arising from any activities.

Tsp - teaspoon Tbsp - tablespoon ml - millilitre l - litre gm - gram 1 cup - 250 millilitre cm - centimetre

Colourful Black

Duration of Experiment: 2 hours

Difficulty Level:

What you need:

Blotting paper

Glass

Ice cream stick

Scotch tape

Black felt pen

Water

What to do:

Step 1. Draw two black lines with the black felt pen at the bottom of two thin strips of blotting paper.

Step 2. Tape the strips to the ice cream stick with the black lines at the top, leaving space between the lines and the stick.

Step 3. Place the stick across the glass.

Step 4. Pour enough water into the glass to touch the bottom of the blotting paper, but not the black line.

Step 5. Take the blotting paper out once the water reaches the top of the blotting paper and dry it.

Step 6. You can see all the colours that black is made of.

SCIENCE AROUND US

Chromatography

In chemistry, chromatography is a process used by scientists to separate the various components of a mixture. Though scientists use more complicated apparatus and put the mixture through many steps, the experiment you just performed is an elementary form of chromatology, which is the study of colour!

What just happened?

The water moved up the filter paper (against the force of gravity) through capillary action due to the tiny pores or tubes on the paper. As the water moved over the black pen lines, some chemicals dissolved better in water and spread up the blotting paper, creating a unique pattern.

Make a Rainbow

Duration of Experiment: 10 mins.

Difficulty Level:

What you need:

Glass

White paper

Water

What to do:

Step 1. Fill three quarters of the glass with water.

Step 2. Take the glass and the paper to your window.

Step 3. Hold the glass above the paper.

Let sunlight pass through the glass and fall on the paper.

Step 4. Adjust your paper a little till you see a mini rainbow on it.

What just happened?

When sunlight passes through water, it refracts or bends, splitting into seven colours. This is what you just created on your paper.

Nail Piano

Duration of Experiment: 30 mins.

Difficulty Level:

What you need:

Small block of wood

7 nails

Hammer

Plank of wood

What to do:

Step 1. Drive the nails into the plank of wood in such a manner that each successive nail is a little further than the one before it, and on an incline.

Step 2. Drive one nail into the small block.

Step 3. Hit the nails on the plank with the single nail to play your 'nail piano'.

Step 4. You can even tune it by driving the nails further in or pulling them out!

What just happened?

Wood is a good conductor of sound. The wood transfers the vibrations caused by hitting one nail with the other.

Water Magnifier

Duration of Experiment: 5 mins.

Difficulty Level:

What you need:

Eye dropper

Transparent plastic square

Water

What to do:

Step 1. Place the plastic square on a page of fine print.

Step 2. Add a drop of water to the centre of the plastic square.

Step 3. Watch how the print is magnified under the drop of water.

What just happened?

The water acts as a lens. The lens bends the light from the image underneath it to your eye, making the image appear larger.

Make Your Own Kaleidoscope

Duration of Experiment: 20 mins.

Difficulty Level:

What you need:

Ruler

Tape

Glass cutter

Sequins

Cardboard

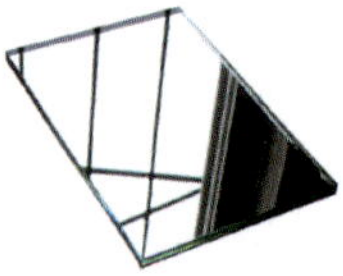

Mirror

What to do:

Step 1. Cut the mirror into three, 4 × 15 cm strips using the glass cutter.

Step 2. Cut the cardboard into three similar strips.

Step 3. Paste the cardboard strips onto the back of the mirror. Tape the three strips together in the form of a triangle.

Step 4. Look at some sequins through the kaleidoscope and rotate it. Enjoy the colourful display.

What just happened?

Light travels in a straight line. But when it hits the mirror, it is reflected. The reflections bounce back and forth from side to side, creating multiple images.

Reading Light

Duration of Experiment: 15 mins.

Difficulty Level:

What you need:

Tape

Scissors

Aluminium foil

Paraffin wax blocks

What to do:

Step 1. Cut a piece of aluminium foil in the same size as the two wax blocks.

Step 2. Tape the foil between the two blocks.

Step 3. Your photometer is ready. If the top block is brighter, the top half of the room is brighter than the bottom half.

What just happened?

Wax is a translucent material. Light can enter it and is reflected back through the block with the help the aluminium foil. Thus, you can measure light intensity by the brightness of the block.

Bending Light

Duration of Experiment: 10 mins.

Difficulty Level:

What you need:

Scissors

Shoe box

Torch

Jar

Water

What to do:

Step 1. Cut a small slit at one end of the shoe box.

Step 2. Fill the jar with water.

Step 3. Put the jar in the box against the slit.

Step 4. Go to a dark room and shine the light from the torch through the slit.

Step 5. Watch the light 'bend'!

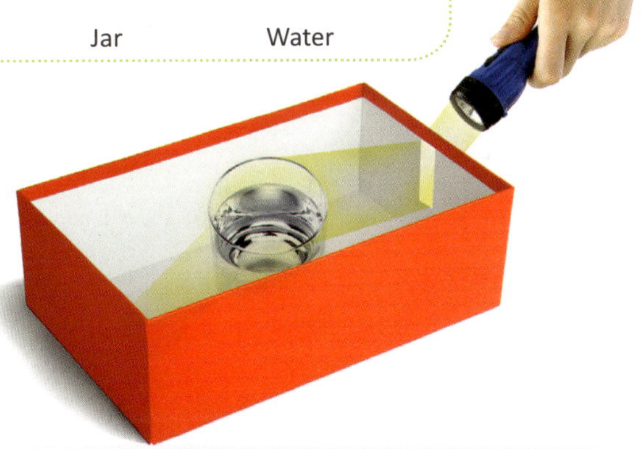

What just happened?

Light 'bends' or refracts because of the different speeds of light in air and water. When light enters water, it bends and does so once again while exiting.

Sound in a Jar

Duration of Experiment: 5 mins.

Difficulty Level:

What you need:

Straw

Clay

Screwdriver

Airtight jar

Buzzer or any small object that creates a continuous sound

What to do:

Step 1. Use the screwdriver to make a hole in the lid of the jar.

Step 2. Set the buzzer off and put it in the jar.

Step 3. Put the straw through the hole in the lid and seal it in place with the clay.

Step 4. Suck all the air out of the jar through the straw. Pinch the straw between breaths to make sure no air escapes.

Step 5. The sound from the buzzer slowly disappears.

What just happened?

Sound needs a medium to travel. There is no sound in a vacuum. Once you sucked all the air out of the jar, you couldn't hear the buzzer.

Black or White?

Duration of Experiment: 45 mins.

Difficulty Level:

What you need:

Glasses

Thermometer

Rubber bands

White and Black paper

Water

What to do:

Step 1. Wrap one glass with white paper, and the other with black paper. Secure both of them with the rubber bands.

Step 2. Fill both glasses halfway with water.

Step 3. Leave them in the sunlight for sometime.

Step 4. Measure the temperature of both. The black glass will be warmer.

What just happened?

Dark surfaces, such as the black paper absorb more light and heat than the lighter ones, such as the white paper.

Twinkle Twinkle Little Star

Duration of Experiment: 30 mins.

Difficulty Level:

What you need:

Pins

Paint brush

Bowl

Water

Aluminium foil

Marbles

Scissors

Blanket

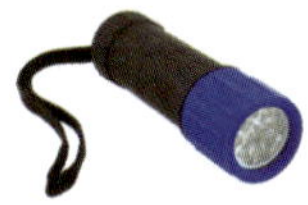

Torch

Black paint

What to do:

Step 1. Cut a circle in the centre of the foil that is as big as the mouth of the torch.

Step 2. Wrap the insides of the bowl with foil with the shiny side facing inwards and the hole facing the bottom.

Step 3. Fill 3/4th of the bowl with water.

Step 4. Put a few marbles in the bowl.

Step 5. Cover the top of the bowl with foil, shiny side facing inwards.

Step 6. Paint the top of this foil black.

Step 7. Make a few holes in the foil with the pins.

Step 8. Cover your head with a thick blanket and shine the torchlight through the bottom of the bowl, where the hole was made. Look at the bowl from the top. You will be able to see 'twinkling stars'.

What just happened?

The light from the torch is reflected by the foil and bounces all over the bowl. However, the marbles come in the way, casting shadows. But as the water moves, the light bends, sometimes reaching your eye and sometimes not. This is exactly how stars twinkle in reality. As the light travels through the different layers of the atmosphere, the light from the stars bend.

Colour-Changing Carnations

Duration of Experiment: 48 mins.

Difficulty Level:

What you need:

Knife

3 White carnations

Food colour

Water

3 glasses of water

What to do:

Step 1. Fill half of each glass with water. Add 30 drops of food colour into three different glasses.

Step 2. Make a fresh diagonal cut at the end of each stem and place each one in a different glass.

Step 3. Within two days, the colour of the carnation petals will change.

What just happened?

The water travels up the stem of the plant into the leaves and flowers, where it makes food. This process is called capillary action.

Make a Kazoo

Duration of Experiment: 20 mins.

Difficulty Level:

What you need:

Pencil

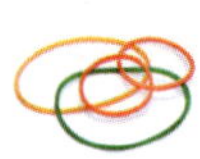

Rubber band

Cardboard tube

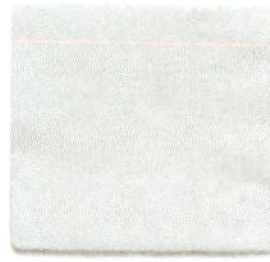

Tissue paper

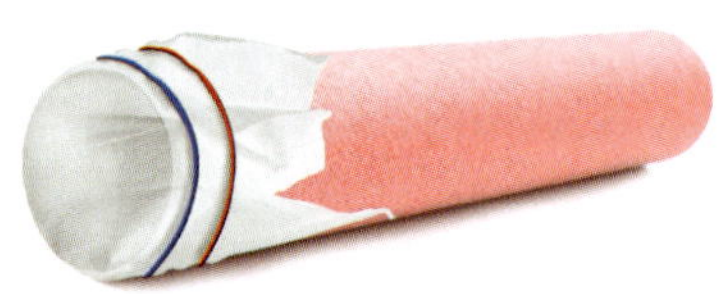

What to do:

Step 1. Place tissue over one end of the cardboard tube. Secure it with a rubber band.

Step 2. Use the pencil to make a hole in the cardboard tube near this end.

Step 3. Hum into the other end of the roll to create a comical sound.

What just happened?

Humming or speaking into the cardboard tube makes the tissue at the bottom vibrate. All these vibrations can only escape through the small hole. This is why the sound is loud.

Sounds of Ruler

Duration of Experiment: 5 mins.

Difficulty Level:

What you need:

Steel ruler

Wooden board

What to do:

Step 1. Press one end of the ruler down on the board, letting the other end protrude over the edge.

Step 2. Push the free end down and let it go.

Step 3. As it vibrates, you will be able to hear a low pitched sound.

What just happened?

All sound is made by vibrations. When you release the ruler, it vibrates, making the noise. The faster the vibrations, the higher the pitch will be.

Strum Away

Duration of Experiment: 15 mins.

Difficulty Level:

What you need:

Rubber bands

Cardboard box

What to do:

Step 1. Stretch the rubber bands over the cardboard box.

Step 2. Pull one rubber band and let it go. Notice the sound.

Step 3. Pull the rubber band a little more and let it go. Notice the difference in sound.

What just happened?

In the first case, the rubber band only vibrated a very short distance, making a weak sound. In the second case, the vibrations were stronger and so was the sound.

Hello!

Duration of Experiment: 10 mins.

Difficulty Level:

What you need:

String

Scissors

2 tin cans

What to do:

Step 1. Cut a long piece of string (around 6 feet).
Step 2. Make a small hole at the bottom of both cans.
Step 3. Thread the string through each can and tie a knot to secure it.
Step 4. Ask a friend to take one can and stand at a distance that makes the string completely tight.
Step 5. Hold your can to your ear.
Step 6. Ask your friend to talk into hers. Then, exchange places and talk into the can and ask your friend to listen.

What just happened?

Speaking into the can creates sound waves that are converted into vibrations at the bottom of the can. These vibrations travel along the string and are converted back into sound waves.

Fruity Fireball

Duration of Experiment: 5 mins.

Difficulty Level:

What you need:

Candle

Orange peel

Matchsticks

Be careful while handling fire and make sure your hands don't get too close to the flame.

What to do:

Step 1. Light the candle.

Step 2. Hold the orange peel next to the candle and squeeze it.

Step 3. Your candle will burst into an impressive fireball as the droplets from the peel fly towards the flame.

What just happened?

There are small compartments in an orange peel that are filled with oil. When you squeeze the peel, these compartments also get squeezed and spray the oil in the direction of the candle, which flames up.

Wailing Ruler

Duration of Experiment: 5 mins.

Difficulty Level:

What you need:

String

Ruler

Nail

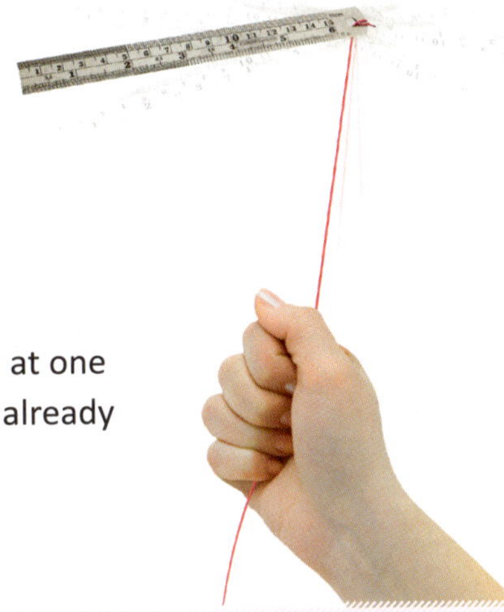

What to do:

Step 1. Use the nail to make a hole at one end of the ruler or use a ruler that already has a hole in it. Tie the string to it.

Step 2. Hold the string and whirl the ruler around.

Step 3. You can hear a low-pitched wailing sound.

What just happened?

When you whirl the ruler fast enough, the speed of the ruler is more than the speed of sound. This creates a sonic boom, which creates the sound.

Roaring Balloon

Duration of Experiment: 5 mins.

Difficulty Level:

What you need:

Coins

Balloon

What to do:

Step 1. Put a rough edged coin into the empty balloon and blow it up.

Step 2. Swirl the balloon around in such away that the coin is rolling against the balloon.

Step 3. You should be able to hear your balloon roar!

What just happened?

The edge of the coin is rough and bounces on the balloon's surface. This causes small vibrations. The noise is magnified by the air in the balloon.

Duck Calls

Duration of Experiment: 10 mins.

Difficulty Level:

What you need:

Scissors

Straw

What to do:

Step 1. Flatten one end of the straw.

Step 2. Cut the flattened end of the straw in the shape of a pointed 'V'.

Step 3. Put the pointed end in your mouth and blow.

Step 4. You can hear a sound like a duck call!

What just happened?

The flaps of the pointed end vibrate very fast against each other when you blow through the straw. These vibrations create the noise.

Straw Flute

Duration of Experiment: 10 mins.

Difficulty Level:

What you need:

Straw

Scissors

What to do:

Step 1. Flatten one end of the straw.

Step 2. Cut the flattened end of the straw into a pointed 'V'.

Step 3. Cut three holes in the straw along the length of the straw.

Step 4. Put the pointed end in your mouth and blow.

Step 5. Close each of the holes and blow. See how the sound differs!

What just happened?

When you blow into the straw, it causes a vibration. The pitch of the sound depends on the time taken by the vibration to travel from one hole to the other. That is why, when you block different holes, the vibration travels different distances, making you hear different sounds!

Candle See-saw

Duration of Experiment: 5 mins.

Difficulty Level:

What you need:

Knife

Needle

Glasses

Candle

What to do:

Step 1. Scrape the wax off one end of the candle. Make sure that the wick is exposed.

Step 2. Push a long needle into the middle of the candle. Balance this on the two glasses.

Step 4. Light both ends of candle.

What just happened?

When a drop of wax melts and falls from one end of the candle, it becomes lighter and rises. When a drop falls from the other end, that rises too. And so it goes on, till the candle is completely burned out.

Glow in the Dark Water

Duration of Experiment: 15 days

Difficulty Level:

What you need:

Highlighter

Black light (available at hardware stores or online)

Water

What to do:

Step 1. Remove the felt from the highlighter and soak it in water for a few minutes.

Step 2. Go to a dark room and turn on the black light near the water.

Step 3. The water will 'glow'.

What just happened?

The dye from the highlighter pens contains phosphorus that turns UV light (light we can't see) into visible light (light we can see). That's why the water glows in the dark when you shine black light on it.

Colourful Crystals

Duration of Experiment: 40 hours

Difficulty Level:

What you need:

Eggshells

Spoon

Alum powder

Water

Food colour

Glue

Measuring cup

What to do:

Step 1. Crack your eggshells into two.

Step 2. Spread a thin layer of glue on the inside.

Step 3. While the glue is still wet, sprinkle it with alum powder. Leave the eggshells in the box to dry overnight.

Step 4. The next day, add five drops of food colour to about two cups of water.

Step 5. Heat the water till it is almost boiling.

Step 6. Pour ¾th cup of alum powder into the water and stir it till all the alum is dissolved. Drop the eggshells into this mixture and let it cool overnight.

Step 7. Pick them up the next morning and enjoy your pretty coloured crystals!

What just happened?

When the water is hot, it is less dense than cold water. Hence, you are able to dissolve more alum powder in the hot water. When the water starts cooling, it becomes denser and there is no space for the alum. So it crystallises in the egg.

Rock Candy

Duration of Experiment: 7 days

Difficulty Level:

What you need:

Food colour

Spoon

Water

2 cups of sugar

Pan

Jar

Wooden chopstick

What to do:

Step 1. Put the water, food colour and sugar in the pan.

Step 2. Bring it to a boil and keep stirring till all the sugar has dissolved.

Step 3. Pour this syrup into the jar and put the wooden chopsticks in it.

Step 4. Leave it untouched for a week. Enjoy your rock candy after that.

What just happened?

The hot water was saturated with sugar. As it cooled, it could not retain the sugar, which crystallised on the chopsticks.

Dancing Goop

Duration of Experiment: 15 mins.

Difficulty Level:

What you need:

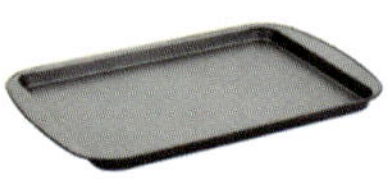

Thin metal cookie sheet

Water

Paint

Speaker

2 cups cornstarch

What to do:

Step 1. Mix water with cornstarch until it achieves the consistency of honey.

Step 2. Spread this mixture on the cookie sheet.

Step 3. Add different coloured paint to the mixture.

Step 4. Place the sheet on a speaker and play loud music.

Step 5. Hold the edges of the sheet and watch your goop dance!

What just happened?

Sound is caused by vibrations. The special texture of the goop made it dance in the presence of these vibrations.

Parachute

Duration of Experiment: 30 mins.

Difficulty Level:

What you need:

Scissors

String

Small toy

Plastic bag

What to do:

Step 1. Cut out an octagon from the plastic bag.

Step 2. Cut a small hole near the edge of each side.

Step 3. Attach 8 pieces of equal-sized string to each of the holes.

Step 4. Tie the pieces of string to the toy and drop your parachute slowly.

What just happened?

When you release the parachute, the weight pulls down on the strings and opens up a large surface area of material that uses air resistance to slow it down.

Upright Broom

Duration of Experiment: 30 mins.

Difficulty Level:

What you need:

Long handle broom

What to do:

Step 1. Find a smooth, hard floor. Place the broom on the floor with the bristles facing down.

Step 2. Keep adjusting the handle by pushing it slightly forward or backward till you can get it to stand on its own.

What just happened?

By making slight adjustments to the handle, you shifted the centre of gravity till it is ideal for the broom to balance without support.

Bottled Beam

Duration of Experiment: 10 mins.

Difficulty Level:

What you need:

Torch

Nails

Water

Bottle

What to do:

Step 1. Make a hole in the side of the bottle near the base using one of the nails.

Step 2. Cover the hole with your finger. Fill the bottle with water.

Step 3. Shine a torch through the other side of the bottle.

Step 4. Move your hand down the stream of water. You should be able to see a spot of light on your hand.

What just happened?

In this case, light does not travel in a straight line and 'bends' to reach your hand. Water acts like a mirror, reflecting light within its stream.

Water Exchange

Duration of Experiment: 10 mins.

Difficulty Level:

What you need:

Red and blue food colouring

Jars

Hot water and cold water

Cardboard

What to do:

Step 1. Fill one jar with hot water. Add blue food colour.

Step 2. Fill the other jar with cold water. Add red food colour.

Step 3. Cover the jar with red coloured water, with the cardboard.

Step 4. Turn the jar with red coloured water over the jar with blue coloured water and take the cardboard piece out.

Step 5. The blue coloured water will move up and the red coloured water will move down.

What just happened?

Hot water has a lower density than cold water, which means that it is lighter. So, the cold water sinks to the bottom and the hot water makes its way up.

Snow Crystal

Duration of Experiment: 48 mins.

Difficulty Level:

What you need:

Pencil

Knife

String

Jar

Boiling water

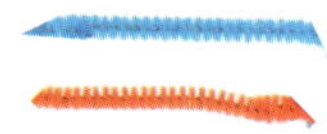
Pipe cleaner

Sugar

What to do:

Step 1. Cut the pipe cleaner into three equal sections.
Step 2. Shape it into a crystal.
Step 3. Tie a string to the middle of the crystal.
Step 4. Tie the opposite end to the pencil.
Step 5. Fill half the jar with boiling water.
Step 6. Keep adding sugar to the water till no more can be dissolved.
Step 7. Hang the snowflake into the jar with the pencil resting on top of it.
Step 8. Leave the snowflake overnight. The next morning, it will be covered with crystals.

SCIENCE AROUND US

Snowflakes
Snowflakes form when water vapour in clouds condenses into ice crystals. Snowflakes have a hexagonal structure, much like the sugar flake you just created! Did you know that no two snowflakes are exactly the same?

What just happened?

Hot water holds more dissolved sugar than cold water. When the solution cools, the water molecules move closer together and it can't hold as much sugar as the hot water could, making the solution very dense. Crystals begin to form on top of each other and you have a crystal snowflake.

Water Slide

Duration of Experiment: 20 mins.

Difficulty Level:

What you need:

Saucer

Different sized books

Plastic sheet

Water

What to do:

Step 1. Place several books vertically.

Step 2. Place the sheet of plastic over them, making sure there are no creases or wrinkles. Place the saucer at the end of the plastic sheet.

Step 3. Let a drop of water fall on the highest part of the slide.

Step 4. It will go down the first slope, up the second and so on, till it reaches the saucer.

What just happened? The speed that the water droplet gained on its way down the slope sustained it as it went up the next slope.

Floating Ketchup

Duration of Experiment: 5 mins.

Difficulty Level:

What you need:

Salt

Ketchup sachet

Plastic bottle

Water

What to do:

Step 1. Fill the plastic bottle with water, and drop the ketchup sachet in it.

Step 2. Add salt to the bottle till the ketchup sachet is just about floating.

Step 3. Put the cap on and squeeze the bottle.

Step 4. The packet should sink when you squeeze it, and float when you release it.

What just happened?

There is an air bubble trapped in the ketchup sachet, which makes it float. Squeezing the bottle reduces the size of the air bubble, making it sink. Once the bottle is released, the air bubble expands, making it float again.

The Lava Cup

Duration of Experiment: 15 mins.

Difficulty Level:

What you need:

Salt

12 drops food colour

Glass

¾ glass water

¼ cup vegetable oil

What to do:

Step 1. Add food colour and vegetable oil to the glass of water.

Step 2. Sprinkle salt on top of the oil.

Step 3. Watch the lava blobs move up and down in your glass!

What just happened?

The oil floats on top of the water because it is lighter than the water. The salt sinks down to the water, taking some oil with it. Once the salt dissolves, the oil goes back up.

Music Box

Duration of Experiment: 30 mins.

Difficulty Level:

What you need:

Scissors

Glue

Large matchbox

Rubber bands

Cardboard

What to do:

Step 1. Cut a right-angled triangle out of the cardboard. The length of the base should be the same as the width of the matchbox.

Step 2. Make four grooves along the hypotenuse.

Step 3. Stick the right-angled triangle across the middle of the matchbox.

Step 4. Stretch the rubber bands over the matchbox. Let the rubber bands rest in the grooves.

Step 5. Pluck each rubber band. Each one will give a different sound.

What just happened?

The different sounds are produced by different vibrations. The more the rubber band is stretched, the higher the pitch will be.

Cool Crystals

Duration of Experiment: 7-8 mins.

Difficulty Level:

What you need:

Woollen thread

Baking soda

Dish

Spoon

2 jars

2 Paper clips

Hot water

What to do:

Step 1. Fill two jars with hot water.

Step 2. Add baking soda until you can't dissolve any more.

Step 3. Attach the two paper clips to the ends of the thread.

Step 4. Suspend it in the jars, as shown.

Step 5. Place a dish under the lowest part of the thread. Crystals form in a week.

What just happened?

The baking soda drips off the lowest point of the thread onto the plate. However, a small amount of the baking soda remains on the thread after each drip.

Crazy Lava Lamp

Duration of Experiment: 30 mins.

Difficulty Level:

What you need:

Antacid tablet

Plastic bottle

Vegetable oil

12 drops food colour

Water

What to do:

Step 1. Fill $\frac{1}{4}$th of the plastic bottle with water and $\frac{1}{4}^{th}$ with the vegetables oil.

Step 2. Wait until the oil and water have separated. Add the food colour into the bottle.

Step 3. Cut the antacid tablet into 5 pieces and drop one of them into the bottle.

Step 4. You should soon be able to see coloured bubbles floating to the top, just like in a real lava lamp.

Step 5. You can even shine a flashlight through the bottom of the bottle to make it look cooler.

SCIENCE AROUND US

Snowflakes

Actual lava lamps contain wax in a clear liquid. The melted wax rises as it gets heated by the bulb at the bottom and falls as it cools. But the basic principle behind your lamp and the fancy ones is exactly the same!

What just happened?

The oil settled on top of the water because of its lower density. The food colouring mixed with the water at the bottom. The piece of antacid tablet released small bubbles of carbon dioxide gas that rose to the top and took some of the coloured water along for the ride.

Bottle Accelerometer

Duration of Experiment: **10 mins.**

Difficulty Level:

What you need:

Cork

String

Thumb tack

1 plastic bottle

Water

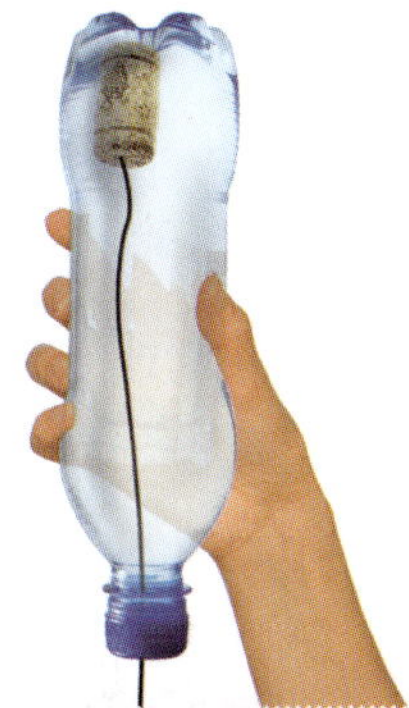

What to do:

Step 1. Attach one end of the string to the cork with the thumb tack.

Step 2. Put this in the bottle of water and screw the cap over the other end of the string.

Step 3. Turn the bottle over and walk around the room. The cork moves in whichever direction you move!

What just happened?

Because water has a greater density, the cork is pushed forward when you walk.

Salty Straws

Duration of Experiment: **15 mins.**

Difficulty Level:

What you need:

6 cups

Salt

Food colour

Straw

Water

What to do:

Step 1. Add 1 teaspoon of salt to the first cup, two to the second and so on.

Step 2. Put a different food colour in each cup.

Step 3. Dip the straw into the first cup.

Step 4. Block the other end of the straw and take it out.

Step 5. Dip it into the second cup and release it.

Step 6. Once water enters the straw, block it again. Repeat steps 4 and 5 for all cups.

What just happened?

The salt changes the density of the water. Since the first cup was the least dense, it remains at the top.

Gummy Bear Expansion

Duration of Experiment: 24 hours

Difficulty Level:

What you need:

Gummy bears

Bowl

Water

What to do:

Step 1. Fill half the bowl with water.
Step 2. Put one gummy bear in it.
Step 3. Leave it overnight.
Step 4. It will become twice its size by the next morning!

What just happened?

Water always flows from areas of lower density to higher density. Gummy bears are very dense, making it easy for them to absorb the water, like a sponge does.

Magic Corn

Duration of Experiment: 15 mins.

Difficulty Level:

What you need:

Unpopped corn

Ball bearing

Ping pong ball

Jar

What to do:

Step 1. Put the ping-pong ball in the jar and fill it with corn.
Step 2. Put the ball bearing on top. Swirl it around.
Step 3. The ball bearing will sink to the bottom and the ping pong ball will come to the surface.

What just happened?

Since the ball bearing has a greater density, it sinks down and the ping-pong ball finds its way up.

Floating Golf Ball

Duration of Experiment: 15 mins.

Difficulty Level:

What you need:

Golf ball

Salt

Plastic container

Water

What to do:

Step 1. Fill half the container with water.

Step 2. Dissolve salt in the container till it can dissolve no more.

Step 3. Place the golf ball on the water. It should float.

Step 4. Add fresh water. The ball remains suspended in the middle of the jar!

What just happened?

The salt water is denser than the golf ball. So, it floats. However, the fresh water is less dense than the ball, which is why it remains suspended.

Falling Water

Duration of Experiment: 15 mins.

Difficulty Level:

What you need:

Styrofoam cup

Sharp pencil

Water

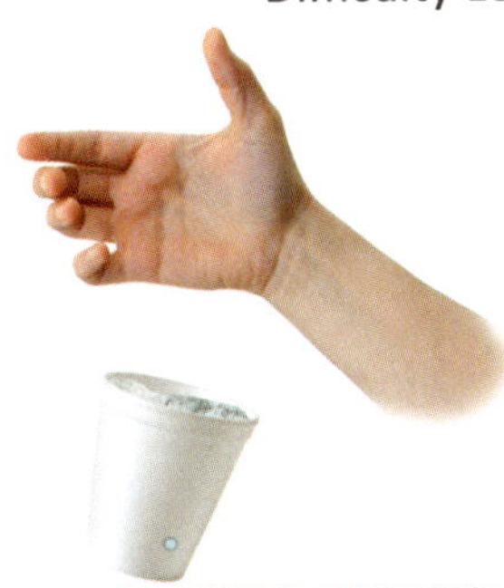

What to do:

Step 1. Use the pencil to make a hole in the side of the cup.

Step 2. Cover the hole with your thumb and fill the glass with water.

Step 3. Take your thumb off the hole. The water leaks out of the hole.

Step 4. Drop the glass. While the glass is falling, the water stops leaking from the hole.

What just happened?

When you're holding the cup in your hand, gravity is pulling on the glass and the water, but only the water moves. This is because you are holding the cup in place. When you drop the glass, gravity is pulling the glass as well as the water at the same rate.

The Static Egg

Duration of Experiment: 30 mins.

Difficulty Level:

What you need:

Pin

Salt

Raw egg

Glue

What to do:

Step 1. Poke a hole at one end of the egg using the pin.

Step 2. Carefully make a slightly bigger hole at the other end by cracking it slightly.

Step 3. Blow through the pinhole so that the inside becomes hollow.

Step 4. Let it dry for a while and glue the pinhole.

Step 5. Through the other end, add a pinch of salt and glue it shut too.

Step 6. Once it has dried, the egg will remain in whatever position you place it.

What just happened?

When you place the egg in a particular position, the salt settles at the bottom. The egg is heavier at the bottom and lighter on top. So it stays in the same position.

Cutting Pear

Duration of Experiment: 15 mins.

Difficulty Level:

What you need:

Pear

Knife

Plate

Cup

Scissors

Cotton thread

Water

What to do:

Step 1. Tie the pear using the cotton thread. Hang it above a table.

Step 2. Fill water in the cup. Hold it under the pear so that the pear is touching the water.

Step 3. Remove the cup from under the pear. Watch where the water droplet is falling.

Step 4. Place a knife with its blade facing the spot where water droplet fell.

Step 5. Now, cut the string so that the pear falls straight on the knife and gets sliced.

What just happened?

Gravity ensured that the pear fell down in a straight line. The force with which it fell ensured that the knife sliced right through it.

Three-layered Float

Duration of Experiment: 30 mins.

Difficulty Level:

What you need:

Honey

Raisins

Oil

Tall glass

Water

Cork

Coin

What to do:

Step 1. Fill ⅓rd of the glass with honey, ⅓rd with oil and the rest with water.

Step 2. Once the substances have settled, drop in the raisins cork and coin into the glass.

Step 3. The cork floats on top, the coin sinks to the bottom, but the raisins remain suspended in the middle!

What just happened?

All three items (raisins, coin and cork) have different densities and float in separate layers according to their density.

Clean Water

Duration of Experiment: 2 hours

Difficulty Level:

What you need:

Woollen string

2 bowls

Thick books

Dirty water

What to do:

Step 1. Stack 3-4 books on a table and place a bowl of dirty water on it.

Step 2. Place an empty bowl next to the books.

Step 3. Put one end of the wool in the dirty water and the other in the empty bowl.

Step 4. After a while, you will see clean drops of water dripping into the empty bowl.

What just happened?

The rope absorbs water from the bowl, but leaves the dirt behind.

OTHER TITLES IN THIS SERIES

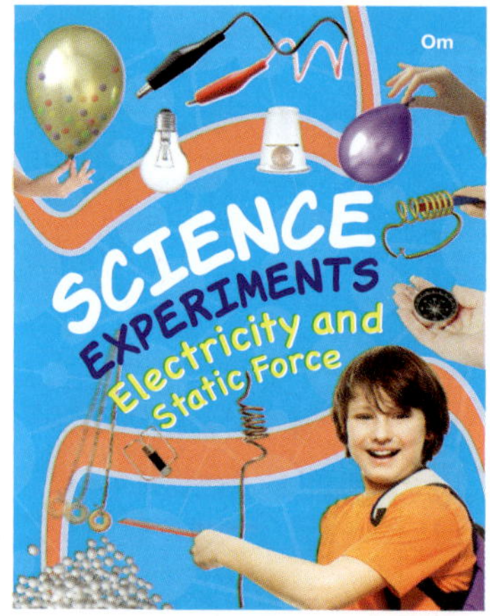

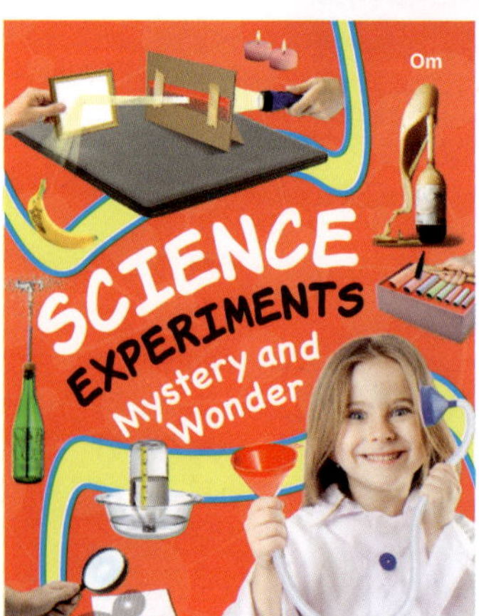

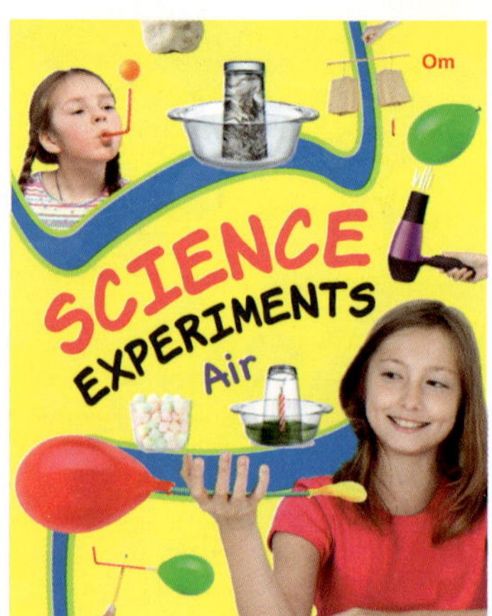

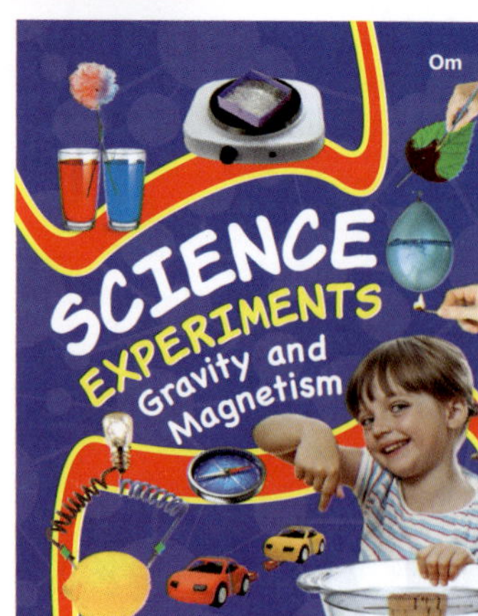